CAPITAL BUDGETING

Toye Adelaja

CAPITAL BUDGETING

INTRODUCTION

Investment in capital project to generate flow of future economic benefits requires huge amount of capital and in order to invest wisely, capital expenditure should be adequately planned and controlled. Such investments include acquisition of equipment, land and building and introduction of new products and so on.

TABLE OF CONTENTS

CHAPTER 1

CAPITAL EXPENDITURE PLANNING AND CONTROL

In this chapter, readers should be able to understand:

(i) Capital Expenditure planning.

(ii) Capital budgeting procedures.

1.0 INTRODUCTION

Capital expenditures are the expenditures incurred on the acquisition of fixed assets and other long-term projects to generate future economic benefits. In this context, capital expenditure is regarded as capital investment. These capital expenditures require huge amount of money, and hence all efforts should be taken to plan and control capital expenditure in order to avoid wasteful spending.

There are cases when the equipment is the major asset that generates income for a company. For example, the aircraft and the ship are the backbone of an airline and shipping company, respectively.

The capital expenditure has to be properly planned, evaluated and controlled.

The future cash flows (economic benefits) have to be properly estimated, and this is the most difficult aspect of the planning and evaluation process. When the company concern has appropriately estimated the future cash flows of each capital investment available, the evaluation of each investment proposal using appropriate investment techniques is the next. Each investment proposal should be evaluated based on its capacity and ability to achieve minimum expected return by the providers of capital.

1.1 Capital Investment Decision or Capital Expenditure planning and Control

Pandy (1989 defined capital expenditure planning and control as "a process of facilitating decision covering expenditure on long-term assets".

Capital expenditure planning and control is an integral part of the corporate planning of an organization. Capital expenditure planning and control is also called capital budgeting or capital investment decision.

Capital budgeting processes include:

i)   Identification of investment opportunities

ii)   Developing cash flow estimation

iii)   Evaluation of the net benefits

iv)   Authorization to spend

v)   Control and monitoring of capital projects

i. Identification of investment opportunities

Investment proposals should be properly identified because once fund is committed to it, it cannot be reversed. An effective investment appraisal technique which should maximize the shareholders' wealth should be used to measure the economic worth of projects.

ii. Development of cash flow estimation

Estimation of cash flow for the future has to be developed, but the future is uncertain. As a result of this uncertainty of the future, development and forecasting of cash flow might be difficult. It is therefore, important to take action necessary to arrive at reliable cash flows.

iii. Evaluation of the net benefits

The method or investment appraisal that will reveal the investment with highest net benefits should be adopted. This means that whatever criterion that is applied should be capable of ranking projects correctly in terms of profitability.

At minimum, the total benefits from the investment selected must be higher than its cost adjusted for time value and risk.

In this particular case, the net present value method is theoretically recommended by experts as it has a true measure of profitability. It ranks projects correctly and is consistent with the wealth maximization criterion. However, other methods in use aside from Net Present Value (NPV), are the payback period, the Internal Rate of Return (IRR), Accounting Rate of Return, and Profitability Index (PI).

In the implementation of a sophisticated evaluation system, the use of minimum required rate of return is necessary. This should be based on the riskiness of cash flows of the investment proposed which is considered to be commonly influenced by the following factors, amongst others:

i.   Inflation

ii.   Government policies

iii.   Project life

iv.   Product demand

v.   Price of raw materials and other inputs

There are some capital budget techniques that are suggested to take care of risks. Some of these include:

1) Simulation techniques
2) Sensitivity analysis

3) Conservative analysis
4) Conservative forecasts
5) Standard Deviation
6) Co-efficient of variation

iv. Authorization to Spend

The approval to incur capital expenditure depends on the peculiarity of each company's organisational chart. However, when huge capital expenditure is involved, the authority for the final approval may rest with the board of directors or the top management level.

The approval authority may be delegated to junior management for certain types of investment projects involving small amounts of capital. Funds are usually appropriated for capital expenditure from the capital budget after the final selection of investment appraisal.

v. Control and Monitoring of capital projects

A capital project reporting system is required to review and monitor the performance of investment projects before and after the completion. This will make it easy to compare actual performances with original estimates.

CHAPTER 2

INVESTMENT APPRAISAL TECHNIQUES

Learning objectives

In this chapter, readers will be able to understand:

(i) Investment appraisal Techniques

(ii) Different situations of investment appraisal

2.0 Investment Appraisal Techniques

There are many methods for selecting investments in long-term assets (capital expenditure). The methods of selecting investments in capital expenditures are called investment appraisal techniques.

The investment appraisal technique which is capable of producing the most valid technique of evaluating investment in a project should be selected and used for the evaluation of investment, or investment technique that will evaluate investment in accordance with the objectives of the shareholders' wealth maximization should be selected.

Investment appraisal techniques can be used in two scenarios.

They are as follows:

1. Investment appraisal techniques under certainty

2. Investment appraisal techniques under uncertainty and risks.

It is necessary to accentuate that expenditure incurred on investment, and benefits expected from an investment should be measured in cash. In this regard, it is the cash flow that is important and not the accounting profit.

Assumptions of Investment Appraisal

The following are the assumptions of investment appraisal:

i.   It is assumed that the opportunity cost (rate of return) of capital project is known.

ii.   it is assumed that the cost of investment or the amount of capital expenditure on investment is known.

iii.   The benefits or cash flow from the investments are known.

2.1 Investment Appraisal Techniques under Certainty

Investment appraisal techniques under certainty are the capital budgeting techniques that are used to assess projects' viability when the outcome of the projects can be predicted with certainty.

Investment appraisal which is also called capital budgeting can be evaluated using various techniques. The capital budgeting techniques under certainty can be grouped into two. They are as follows:

1. Non-Discounted Cash Flow Techniques

a. Payback Period
b. Accounting Rate of Return (ARR)

2. Discounted Cash Flow Techniques

a. Net Present Value (NPV)
b. Internal Rate of Return
c. Profitability Index
d. Discounted Payback Period

CHAPTER 3

NON-DISCOUNTED CASH FLOW TECHNIQUES

Learning Objectives

After studying this chapter, you should be able to:

(i) Evaluate capital projects using Pay Back Period Technique.

(ii) Evaluate capital project using Accounting Rate of Return (ARR) Technique.

Non-Discounted Cash Flow Techniques

a)   Payback Period

This technique pays attention to the shortness of the project; it means the shorter the period of recovery of initial investment or capital outlay, the more acceptable the project becomes. It shows the number of years in which the initial investment will be recovered from the cash inflows of the investment.

CIMA defines payback period as the period usually expressed in years, in which the cash outflows will equate the cash inflows of a project.

Decision rule

If the payback period calculated for a period is less than the standard payback period set by the management, the project would be accepted. If not, it would be rejected.

If mutually exclusive projects are involved, whereby only one of the projects can be undertaken, the rule is to accept the project with the shorter payback period.

Advantages of Payback Period
1) It is simple to calculate and understand
2) It is less exposed to uncertainty since it only focuses on shortness of a project
3) It is a fast screening technique especially for a firm that has liquidity problems

Disadvantages of Payback Period
1) It does not take into consideration the time value of money
2) It does not take accounts of cash flows earned after the payback period.
3) It does not take into consideration the risks associated with each project.

ILLUSTRATION 1

Mr. Smith runs a manufacturing business. The project involves an immediate cash outlay of $20,000. He estimated that the net cash flows from the project will be as follows:

Years	Cash flow ($)
1	2,000
2	4,000
3	22,000
4	8,000

Calculate Mr. Smith payback period for the project. The company's required payback period is fixed at 2years and 5months.

Solution

Years	Cash flow ($)	Cumulative cash flow ($)
0	-20,000	-20,000
1	2,000	-18,000
2	4,000	-14,000
3	22,000	
4	8,000	

Procedures:

Deduct cash inflow for each year from the initial outlay (cash outflow) until the whole cash outflow has been exhausted.

Payback period = 2years + $\dfrac{14,000}{22,000}$ ×12 months

= 2years and 7.6 months

Decision rule

Using the payback period, accept project that has shorter payback period than the company's required payback period.

This project should be rejected because its payback period (2 years and 7.6 months) is higher that the company's set payback period (2years and 5months).

ILLUSTRATION 2

PZY Ltd, a manufacturing company, is faced with the problem of choosing between two mutually exclusive projects.

Project A requires a cash outlay of $25,000 and generates a net cash flow of $10,000 per year for 4 years.

Project B requires a cash outlay of $15,000 and generates net cash flow of $6,500, $5,500, $4,000, $5,000 over its life of 4 years.

Which one of the projects should be accepted?

Solution

Project A

Payback period = $\dfrac{\text{Initial outlay}}{\text{Annual Net Cash flow}}$

$$= \dfrac{\$25,000}{\$10,000}$$

$$= 2.5$$

$$= 2 \text{ years} + 0.5 \times 12 \text{months}$$

$$= 2 \text{ years and 6months}$$

Project B

Years	Cash flow ($)	Cumulative cash flow ($)
0	-15,000	-15,000
1	6,500	-8,500
2	5,500	-3,000
3	4,000	
4	5,000	

Payback period = 2 years + $\dfrac{3,000}{4,000}$

$$= 2 + 0.75 \times 12 \text{months}$$

$$= 2 \text{years and 9months}$$

Decision:

Accept project A and reject project B because project A has earlier pay back period than project B.

b)   **Accounting Rate of Return**

The accounting rate of return (ARR) is derived from the concept of return on capital employed (ROCE) or return on capital invested (ROI). It uses the accounting information provided by the financial statements to measure the profitability of an investment. The formula for the calculation of ARR is mentioned below:

$$ARR = \frac{\text{Average profit after tax}}{\text{Average investment}}$$

Note: Average profit after tax is the total profit after tax divided by number of years of the project.

Decision Rule:

The rule is to accept all projects that have higher Accounting Rate of Return than the company's predetermined rate.

Where mutually exclusive projects are involved, the rule is to accept the project that has highest ARR.

Advantages of Accounting Rate of Return

1.   It is easy to calculate
2.   It is easy to understand and use
3.   It incorporates the entire stream of income in calculating projects' profitability.

Disadvantages of Accounting Rate of Return

1.   The averaging of income ignores the time value of money.
2.   It uses accounting profits in appraising the projects.
3.   It does not take into consideration the risk associated with each project as well as the attitude of the management of the company to risk.

ILLUSTRATION 1

Otega recently convinced his friends and relations to grant him a loan of $100,000, which he intends to invest in a farming project. He estimates that the project will yield the following returns annually for next five consecutive years.

Years	$
1	30,000
2	30,000
3	40,000
4	30,000
5	20,000

There were no expectations of scrap values at the end of the fifth year and the project is to be evaluated using Accounting Rate of Return.

Note:

The company's predetermined minimum acceptable ARR is 68%.

You are required to provide the accounting rate of return for the project on the assumption that the annual returns are profits after tax.

Solution:

$$ARR = \frac{\text{Average profit after tax}}{\text{Average investment}} \times 100\%$$

Total annual investment:

$
30,000
30,000
40,000

30,000
20,000
150,000

Average profit after tax = $\frac{150,000}{5}$

$$= \$30,000$$

Average investment $= \$100,000/2$

$$= \$50,000$$

ARR $= \frac{\$30,000}{\$50,000} \times 100\%$

$= 0.6 \times 100\%$

$= 60\%$

Decision Rule:

a) The rule is to invest in all projects whose accounting rate of return are higher than the company's predetermined minimum Accounting Rate of Return.

b) Where there are mutually exclusive projects, the project that has highest ARR should be accepted.

From the solution above, the ARR calculated from the project above is 60%. This is lower than the company's predetermined minimum rate of return (68%). As a result of this, the project should be rejected because it generates lower ARR than the company's predetermined ARR.

CHAPTER 4

CONCEPTS IN CAPITAL BUDGETING DECISION

Learning Objectives

In this chapter, readers will be able to understand:

(i) Concept of time value of money

(ii) Concept of annuity

(iii) Concept of perpetuity

(iv) Concept of relevant cash flow

Concepts in Capital Budgeting Decision

In order to facilitate the understanding of NPV and IRR, we shall explain some basic concepts as they apply to capital budgeting decisions. The concepts are as follows:

a) Concept of time value of money

b) Concept of annuity

c) Concept of perpetuity

d) Concept of relevant cash flows

4.1   Concept of Time Value of Money

Time value of money states that an amount of money now will be greater than the same amount in the future. $1 today is greater than $1 in the future.

Where future value of an amount invested is given, what is the amount invested to generate the future value being given? That is, what is the present value of the future amount given?

In arriving at the present value of the future value, returns or interest on the money invested must be forgone.

This concept is based on compound interest formula.

$$Fv = Pv(1+r)^n$$

Where:

Fv = future value of money receivable in a period
Pv = principal or present value
r = the rate of interest or cost of capital
n = number of years

Pv can be made a subject of the formula in the formula above.

$$Pv = \frac{Fv}{(1+r)^n}$$

$$Pv = Fv(1+r)^{-n}$$

Where $(1+r)^{-n}$ is the discount factor.

ILLUSTRATION

Calculate the present value of $10,000 receivable in 5 years time if the interest rate is 10%.

$$Pv = Fv(1+r)^{-n}$$

$$= 10,000(1+0.1)^{-5}$$

$$= \$10,000 \times 0.6209$$

$$= \$6,209$$

4.2 Concept of Annuity

An annuity is a constant sum of money receivable or payable over a specific period of time.

The present value of annuity can be calculated using the formula below:

$$Pv = A\frac{(1 - (1+r)^{-n})}{r}$$

Where:

Pv = Present value of annuity
A = The constant or equal annual sum
r = rate of interest or cost of capital
n = number of years

ILLUSTRATION

Calculate the present value of $1,000 receivable every year for 5 years at the interest rate of 10% per annum.

$$Pv = A\frac{(1 - (1+r)^{-n})}{r}$$

$$Pv = 1,000 \times \frac{(1 - (1+0.1)^{-5})}{0.1}$$

$$= 1,000 \times \frac{(1 - (1.1)^{-5})}{0.1}$$

$$= \$3,791$$

4.3 Concept of Perpetuity

Concept of Perpetuity is described as a situation in which constant sum of money is saved or withdrawn for an indefinite time. It can also be defined as a perpetual annuity.

The formula for calculating present value of perpetual annuity is described below:

$$Pv = A \times 1/r$$

Where:

Pv = Present value of annuity
A = The constant or equal annual sum
r = rate of interest or cost of capital

ILLUSTRATION

Calculate the present value of $1,000 receivable every year for indefinite period at the interest rate of 10% per annum.

$$Pv = A \times I/r$$

$$= \$1,000 \times 1/0.1$$

$$= \$10,000$$

4.4 Relevant cash Flow

Relevant cash flows are inflow and outflow of cash whose inclusion in or exclusion from investment decision can affect the overall investment decision. This simply means that funds that have already been committed will not be considered while evaluating your project.

Where the present value is used, we state that the cash flows used are discounted cash flow. The discounted cash flow techniques such as NPV and IRR that are used for evaluation of capital projects, recognise only relevant cash flow of a project.

In order to assess a project properly, we need to determine the relevant costs. This is done by taking the following steps:

a) Determine the kind of decision to be taken, for example, accept or reject a project, abandon and replace a project line, scrap a product line, and make or buy an item.

b) Any cash flow that will be influenced or affected by (a) above is relevant.

c) Do not focus your attention only on the project that is being evaluated only, but consider its effects on the other operations of the company. This is called opportunity cost concept which can be a function of cost or revenue thus:

i.   If the decision will result in additional expenses or increased running costs in other operations of the company, then the expenses or costs must be included as relevant cash outflows in the original decision in (a) above

ii.   Similarly, if the project being evaluated will result in additional contributions or savings from other operations of the company, then those savings must be treated as relevant cash inflows in the evaluation of decisions in (a) above.

d) The following are not relevant for projects' evaluation:
i.   all appropriations, reserves and other non cash items.
ii.   All fixed costs except incremental or attributable fixed costs
iii. All historical or sunk or past costs
iv.   Cost of carrying out research and development

Additional Assumptions of capital budgeting are as follows:

i.   The period in which capital or fund is invested should be tagged as year zero in any investment appraisal. It is always at the beginning of investments in year 1, and it is to be taken as a year on its own, this is year zero.

ii.   All other cash flows after year zero are assumed to arise at the end of the year to which they relate. For example, if the accounting year end of a business is December 31, it means that cash flows will occur at December 31 of each year.

CHAPTER 5

DISCOUNTED CASH FLOW TECHNIQUES

Learning Objectives

After studying this chapter, you should be able to:

      i. Distinguish between NPV and IRR

     ii. Evaluate capital projects using discounted cash flow techniques

    iii. Know IRR modification

Discounted Cash Flow Techniques

5.1. Net Present Value

Net present value is one of the discounted cash flow techniques that emphasizes on time value of money. It is the net contribution of a project to its owners' wealth, that is, the present value of future cash flows minus the present value of initial capital invested.

All cash flows are discounted to their present value using the required rate of return. The formula for calculating NPV can be written as follows:

$$NPV = [C_1 \times (1+r)^{-1} + C_2 \times (1+r)^{-2} \ldots C_n \times (1+r)^{-n}] - C_0$$

$C_1 \, C_2 \ldots$ represents cash inflows in year 1, 2...n

r represents the opportunity cost of capital

C_0 is the initial cost of the investment

r represents the opportunity cost of capital

$(1+r)^{-n}$ is the discounting factor for each year

Advantages of NPV

(i) It recognises the time value of money

(ii) It includes all the cash flow involved in the entire life of a project in its calculation.

(iii) it is more useful than the IRR for a decision making under capital rationing.

Disadvantages of NPV

(i) It is more difficult to calculate than PBP and ARR.

(ii) It relies heavily on the correct estimation of cost of capital, that is, where errors occur in the cost of capital used for discounting the decision, using the NPV would be misleading.

ILLUSTRATION 1

A machine costing $20,000 will provide annual net cash inflow of $6,000 for six years at a cost of capital of 10%.

You are required to:

   i. Calculate the net present value (NPV) of the machine

   ii. Should the machine be purchased?

Solution

years	Cash flow ($)	DCF (10%)	PV ($)
0	-20,000	1	-20,000
1	6,000	0.9091	5,455
2	6,000	0.8265	4,959
3	6,000	0.7513	4,508
4	6,000	0.683	4,098
5	6,000	0.6209	3,725
6	6,000	0.5645	3,387
		NPV	6,132

(ii) Decision: The machine should be purchased because the NPV is positive, that is NPV > 0

Alternatively, annuity as earlier explained in the concept of annuity can also be used to discount the above cash flow and solve the question since the same amount ($6,000) is being expected throughout the years under consideration. The NPV of the project can be calculated as follow:

The discount factor from year 1 to 6 is

$$= \frac{1- (1+r)^{-n}}{r}$$

$$= \frac{1- (1+ 0.1)^{-6}}{0.1}$$

$$= 4.3553$$

Years	Cash flow($)	DCF (10%)	PV($)
0	-20,000	1	-20,000
1 to 6	6,000	4.3553	26,131.8
		NPV	6,132

NOTE:

Where constant cash flows are generated from a project, annuity formula (discount factor) should be used to discount the cash flows.

Decision Rule:

Accept all projects that produce positive Net Present value (NPV)

Accept if NPV > 0
Reject if NPV < 0
May accept or reject if NPV = 0

5.2. Internal Rate of Return (IRR)

The IRR is that cost of capital that will produce NPV of zero when applied to a project. It is a breakeven point cost of capital. It is also the cost of capital or discount rate that will equate the total cash outflow to the total cash inflow of a project.

In order to generate the cost of capital (IRR) that will produce Zero NPV, the following procedures may be followed:

a) Generate two (2) opposite values of NPV (+ and – value) using two different discount rates earlier calculated. It should be noted that the higher the discount rate, the lower the NPV, and the lower the discount rate the higher the NPV.

b) The above two opposite NPV and the two different discount rates may be applied in the formula below:

$$IRR = Lr + \frac{NPVLr}{NPVLr - (- NPVHr)} \times (Hr - Lr)$$

Where:

Lr = Lower rate of return
Hr = Higher rate of return
$NPVLr$ = Net present value of lower rate of return
$NPVHr$ = Net present value of higher rate of return

Advantages of IRR

i. It recognizes time value of money

ii. It is consistent with shareholders' wealth maximization objectives.

iii. It considers all cash flows occurring over the entire life of a project.

Disadvantages of IRR

i. It is more difficult to calculate than the other methods

ii. In some cases, it fails to indicate a correct choice between mutually exclusive projects.

iii. Sometimes, it yields multiple rates

iv. It can give misleading and inconsistent results when the NPV of a project does not decline with discount rates.

ILLUSTRATION 1

A machine costing $20,000 will provide annual net cash inflow of $6,000 for six years at a cost of capital of 10%. Calculate the Internal rate of Return of the machine.

Solution

Step1: calculation of the rate that generates +NPV

Years	Cash flow($)	DCF (10%)	PV ($)
0	-20,000	1	-20,000
1	6,000	0.9091	5,455
2	6,000	0.8265	4,959
3	6,000	0.7513	4,508
4	6,000	0.683	4,098
5	6,000	0.6209	3,725
6	6,000	0.5645	3,387
		NPV	6,132

Step 2: calculation of the rate that generates – NPV

Years	Cash flow ($)	DCF (20%)	PV ($)
0	-20,000	1	-20,000
1	6,000	0.8333	5,000
2	6,000	0.6944	4,166
3	6,000	0.5787	3,472
4	6,000	0.4823	2,894
5	6,000	0.4019	2,411
6	6,000	0.3349	2,009
		NPV	-47

The formula can then be applied here:

$$IRR = Lr + \frac{NPVLr}{NPVLr - (-NPVHr)} \times (Hr - Lr)$$

$$IRR = 10\% + \frac{6,132}{6,132 - (-47)} \times (20 - 10)\%$$

IRR = 19.92%

Decision Rule:

Accept all projects whose IRR are greater than the company's cost of capital.

i.e. Accept if $r > k$

Reject if $r < k$

May accept or reject if $r = k$

Where r = internal rate of return and k = cost of capital of the company

Where mutually exclusive projects are involved, the rule is to accept project that produces highest IRR.

5.3. Profitability Index

Profitability Index can be calculated using the following formula:

$$PI = \frac{NPV \text{ of a project}}{Initial \text{ cash outlay}}$$

Or

$$PI = \frac{PV \text{ of a project}}{Initial \text{ outlay}}$$

Advantages of PI

i. It recognizes the time value of money.

ii. It is generally consistent with wealth maximization principle.

iii. It is a variation of the NPV method and requires the same computation as in the NPV method.

Disadvantages of PI

i. It cannot be used to evaluate mutually exclusive projects or dependent projects.

ii. It can only be used under simple situation.

ILLUSTRATION 1

A machine costing $20,000 will provide annual net cash inflow of $6,000 for six years at a cost of capital of 10%. Calculate profitability index of the project.

Solution

years	Cash flow($)	DCF(10%)	PV ($)
0	-20,000	1	-20,000
1	6,000	0.9091	5,455
2	6,000	0.8265	4,959
3	6,000	0.7513	4,508
4	6,000	0.683	4,098
5	6,000	0.6209	3,725
6	6,000	0.5645	3,387
		NPV	6,132

PI = $\underline{\text{NPV of the project}}$
       Initial Outlay

PI = $\dfrac{\$6,132}{\$20,000}$

PI = 0.3066

PI = 0.31

OR

PI = $\underline{\text{PV of the project}}$
       Initial Outlay

PI = $\dfrac{\$6,132 + \$20,000}{\$20,000}$

PI = $\dfrac{\$26,132}{\$20,000}$

PI = 1.31

Decision rule:

Accept all projects whose PI is positive or greater than 1

May accept or reject if PI of a project = 0

5.4. Discounted Payback Period Technique (DPPT)

This technique is aimed at overcoming the problem of the time value of money by incorporating into its calculation, the discount factor. In the discounted payback period method, the cash flows are discounted and used in the calculation of payback period.

Advantages of Discounted Payback Period Technique

i.   It recognizes time value of money

ii. It emphasizes on the shortness of a project to payback the initial outlay.
iii. It has all the advantages of payback period aside from the fact that it recognizes time value of money.

Disadvantages of Discounted Payback Period

i.   It does not take into consideration the cash inflow earned after the payback period.

ii. It does not consider a risk associated with each project and the attitude of the company to the risk.

ILLUSTRATION 1

A machine will cost $60,000 and will produce an annual net cash inflow of $20,000 for five years. The opportunity cost of capital is 10 percent.

Calculate the discounted payback period of the machine.

SOLUTION

Step 1

Years	Cash flows	DF (10%)	PV
	$		$
0	-60,000	1	(60,000)

1	20,000	0.9091	18,182
2	20,000	0.8265	16,530
3	20,000	0.7513	15,026
4	20,000	0.683	13,660
5	20,000	0.6209	12,418

Step 2

Years	Cash flow	Cumulative cash flow
	$	$
0	(60,000)	(60,000)
1	18,182	(41,818)
2	16,530	(25,288)
3	15,026	(10,262)
4	13,660	
5	12,418	

Discounted Payback Period:

$$= 3\text{years} + \frac{10,262}{13,660} \times 12\text{months}$$

$$= 3\text{years and 9months}$$

5.5. Controversy between IRR and NPV

An "accept" or "reject" decision is one where each project may be accepted or rejected independent of what happens to other projects. NPV and IRR will always give the conclusion when applied to those projects.

In the case of mutually exclusive projects, the two methods will sometimes lead to different rankings. The conclusion here is that NPV based on discounting the return at equity cost of capital, always gives a correct ranking. The reason is that NPV indicates the immediate gain in market capitalization to equity investors.

NOTE:

NPV prevails if there is a conflict between IRR and NPV.

5.5.1. Modification of IRR

The IRR can be modified for any of the following reasons:

  b) Where the cash flows are unconventional
  c) Where projects are mutually exclusive.

However, the situation above can be taken care of by the following two methods:

  a) Extended Yield method
  b) Incremental Yield method

a)   Extended Yield Method
By this method, we modify the IRR technique in order to produce a unique IRR rather than multiple IRR. The following steps may be applied:
i. Convert the unconventional cash flows into conventional cash flows by discounting all future cash flows backward at the given cost of capital until they are fully absorbed by the positive cash flows (cash inflows) or they become year zero cash flow.

ii. Calculate the IRR of the revised (conventional) cash flows in the normal way. This is the required IRR.

(b)   Incremental Yield Method

Where projects are mutually exclusive, it means that we cannot undertake all the projects. We must undertake only one which means that acceptance of only one project is equivalent to rejection of all other projects.

IRR will produce conflicting result with NPV where mutually exclusive projects are involved because IRR does not recognize the scale or size of investments.

As a result of this, we must modify the cash flow of mutually exclusive projects, if we are mandated to evaluate them using IRR. Hence, the method for this modification is called INCREMENTAL YIELD APPROACH. Under this method, revise the cash flow to generate different or incremental cash flow. Thereafter, we calculate the IRR of these incremental cash flow and base our decision for project selection on the project that generate this incremental cash flow (i.e. the project that was kept constant)

Steps for Calculating Incremental IRR:

The following steps are to be followed in calculating the Incremental IRR.

a) Calculate the incremental cash flow by keeping one project constant (i.e. subtracting cash flow of a project from the cash flow of the project that was kept constant. e.g. project A-B if incremental cash flows are generated from A-B then A must be kept constant.

b) Calculate the IRR of the incremental cash flows in the normal way.

c) If the IRR of the incremental cash flows is greater than the company's cost of capital, then the project whose cash flow is kept constant should be accepted.

Example

Aplic Ltd's two accountants are in disagreement as to which of two mutually exclusive projects to undertake. One has based his conclusions on an IRR computation of the projects, the other based his own conclusion on NPV calculation of the projects. The required rate of return for the company is 10%.

The first project requires an investment of $705,200 and will generate net cash flows of $150,000 per annum for 10years. The second project only requires $433,900 to be invested to generate $200,000 for 10years.
Required:

a) Produce the computation of the two accountants

b) Calculate IRR, by using incremental IRR

c) If the alternative investment rate was 14%, which of the two projects would be accepted?

Solution:

a) First Accountant's computation

Calculation of NPV for Project A

Years	Cash flow $	D.F (10%)	PV $
0	-705,200	1	(705,200)
1 to 10	150,000	6.1446	921,690
		NPV	216,490

The present value for project A is + $216,490.

Calculation of NPV for project B

Years	Cash flow $	D.F (10%)	PV $

0	-433,900	1	(433,900)
1 to 10	100,000	6.1446	614,460
		NPV	180,560

The Net Present Value of project B is +$180,560.

Decision under NPV

According to the accountant that based is decision on the outcome of computation of NPV, Project A should be accepted. The reason is that project A has +NPV of $216,490 which is greater than + NPV of $180,560.

Second accountant's computation:

Calculation of NPV for Project A

Years	Cash flow $	D.F (10%)	PV $
0	-705,200	1	(705,200)
1 to 10	150,000	6.1446	921,690
		NPV	216,490

IRR for project A

Use higher rate of return to generate negative NPV.

Years	Cash flow $	D.F (20%)	PV $
0	-705,200	1	(705,200)
1 to 10	150,000	4.1925	628,875
		NPV	(76,325)

IRR for project A

$$IRR = Lr + \frac{NPVLr}{NPVLr - (-NPVHr)} \times (Hr - Lr)$$

$$= 10\% + \frac{216,490}{216,490 - (-76,325)} \times (20 - 10)\%$$

$$= 0.1 + \frac{216,490}{292,815} \times 0.1$$

$$= 0.1 + 0.0739$$

$$= 0.1739$$

$$= 17.39\%$$

IRR for project B

Rate of return that generates + NPV

Years	Cash flow $	D.F (10%)	PV $
0	-433,900	1	(433,900)
1 to 10	100,000	6.1446	614,460
		NPV	180,560

Use higher rate of return to generate Negative NPV

Years	Cash flow $	D.F (20%)	PV $
0	-433,900	1	(433,900)
1 to 10	100,000	4.1925	419,250

$$\text{NPV} \qquad (14{,}650)$$

$$\text{IRR} = \text{Lr} + \frac{\text{NPVLr}}{\text{NPVLr} - (-\text{NPVHr})} \times (\text{Hr} - \text{Lr})$$

$$= 10\% + \frac{180{,}560}{180{,}560 - (-14{,}650)} \times (20 - 10)\%$$

$$= 10\% + \frac{180{,}560}{195{,}210} \times 10\%$$

$$= 0.1 + 0.92495 \times 0.1$$

$$= 0.1 + 0.092495$$

$$= 0.1925$$

$$= 19.25\%$$

Accountant that based his decision on the outcome of IRR will accept project B and reject project A. This is in contrary to the decision of accountant that based is decision on the outcome of NPV.

NOTE:

Whenever there is a controversy between NPV and IRR, NPV should prevail.

b) Computation of IRR, using incremental IRR

Years	A Cash flow $	B Cash flow $	Incremental cash flow(A - B) $
0	-705,200	-433,900	(271,300)
1 to 10	150,000	100,000	50,000

Rate of return that generates positive NPV:

Years	Incremental cash flow(A - B) $	D.F(10%)	PV $
0	(271,300)	1	(271,300)
1 to 10	50,000	6.1446	307,230
		NPV	35,930

Rate of return that generates Negative NPV:

Years	Incremental cash flow(A - B) $	D.F(20%)	PV $
0	(271,300)	1	(271,300)
1 to 10	50,000	4.1925	209,625
		NPV	(61,675)

$$IRR = Lr + \frac{NPVLr}{NPVLr - (-NPVHr)} \times (Hr - Lr)$$

$$= 10\% + \frac{35{,}930}{35{,}930 - (-61{,}675)} \times (20\text{-}10)\%$$

$$= 0.1 + 0.3681 \times 0.1$$

$$= 0.1 + 0.03681$$

$$= 0.1368$$

$$= 13.68\%$$

Decision:

Since the IRR of the incremental cash flows is greater than the company's cost of capital, it means project A, which was held constant, should be accepted. This decision is the same as the decision of the NPV.

C) If the investment rate is now 14%, it means the decision to accept project A will no more hold as the incremental IRR is less than the cost of capital of 14%. Therefore, project B, now looks more attractive and should be accepted.

CHAPTER 6

COMPLEX INVESTMENT DECISIONS

Learning Objectives

After studying this chapter, you should be able to:

    i. Evaluate capital projects with different lives.

    ii. Evaluate capital projects involving replacement and abandoning decisions

    iii. Evaluate capital project involving inflation.

6.0.   Complex Investment Decisions

Many companies are faced with complex investment decision in a practical situation. Some of the situations include choosing among investments with different lives, deciding about the replacements of an existing fixed asset and evaluating investments under inflation or capital rationing. The NPV rule can be extended to handle such situations.

6.1.   Projects with Different Lives

Where mutually exclusive projects that have the same lives are being considered, the project with the highest NPV should be accepted. However, where mutually exclusive projects being considered have different lives, the use of the NPV rule without accounting for the differences in the projects' lives, may fail to indicate the correct choice. In this situation, there is need to evaluate the projects for an equal period of time to be able to arrive at a reasonable decision.

ILLUSTARATION 6.1a

A company has to choose between two grinding machines; machine Y and machine Z which are of different designs but perform the same functions. Machine Y would involve an initial cash outlay of $2,400 and operating cash expenses of $800 per year for 6 years. On the other hand, machine Z would involve an initial cash outlay of $2,000 and operating cash expenses of $1,000 per year for 3 years. If the opportunity cost of capital is 14 percent, which of the two machines should be accepted?

Hint:

The cash flows above are operating expenses, and hence they have negative figures. Initial outlay should be deducted from the present value of these operating expenses which are in negative figures. In a nutshell, it means that a negative figure minus any figure, equals negative figure. For example:

- 10 - 18 = - 28

SOLUTION

Machine Y

Years	cash flow	DF (14%)	PV
	$		$
0	(2,400)	1	(2,400)
1	(800)	0.877	(702)
2	(800)	0.769	(615)
3	(800)	0.675	(540)
4	(800)	0.592	(474)
5	(800)	0.519	(415)
6	(800)	0.456	(365)
		NPV	(5,510)

Machine Z

Years	cash flow	DF (14%)	PV
	$		$
0	(2,000)	1	(2,000)
1	(1,000)	0.877	(877)
2	(1,000)	0.769	(769)
3	(1,000)	0.675	(675)
		NPV	(4,321)

If the difference in the project lives is disregarded, machine Z will be chosen since it has lower present value of costs. This is not a good decision for a company taking into consideration that machine Y will last for 6 years and machine Z will last for 3 years and will need to be replaced at the end of the third year.

ILLUSTRATION 6.1b

Using illustration 6.1a and assuming that machine M is replaced at the end of the 3rd year at the same initial outlay and same operating expenses and life expectancy, the new position would be as follows:

Machine Y

Years	cash flow	DF (14%)	PV
	$		$
0	(2,400)	1	(2,400)
1	(800)	0.877	(702)
2	(800)	0.769	(615)
3	(800)	0.675	(540)
4	(800)	0.592	(474)
5	(800)	0.519	(415)
6	(800)	0.456	(365)
		NPV	(5,510)

Machine Z

Years	cash flow	DF (14%)	PV
	$		$
0	(2,000)	1	(2,000)
1	(1,000)	0.877	(877)
2	(1,000)	0.769	(769)
3	(3,000)	0.675	(2,025)
4	(1,000)	0.592	(592)
5	(1,000)	0.519	(519)
6	(1,000)	0.456	(456)
		NPV	(7,238)

By the end of year 6, machine Y will need to be replaced for the first time while machine Z would need to be replaced the second time. When the NPVs of the two machines are compared at the end of year 6, machine Y would be chosen. It is clearly shown here that the use of simple NPV rule will produce wrong decision when two projects with different lives are considered.

It is advisable to put into consideration the project lives when taking the decision. The best method of evaluating these types of projects is called Annual Equivalent Value.

Annual Equivalent Value (AEV) is the NPV of an investment divided by annuity factor given its rate and discounts.

$$AEV = \frac{NPV}{Annuity\ Factor}$$

Note:

Annuity factor is the sum of the discounting factor starting from year 1 up to the discounting factor of the last year of the project.

This method can be best used where there is absent of inflation as it is quicker and less cumbersome than any other method.

ILLUSTRATION 6.1c

Using illustration 6.1a, the result will be as follows:

Machine Y

Years	cash flow	DF (14%)	PV
	$		$
0	(2,400)	1	(2,400)
1	(800)	0.877	(702)
2	(800)	0.769	(615)
3	(800)	0.675	(540)
4	(800)	0.592	(474)
5	(800)	0.519	(415)
6	(800)	0.456	(365)
		3.888	(5,510)

Machine Z

Years	cash flow	DF (14%)	PV
	$		$
0	(2,000)	1	(2,000)
1	(1,000)	0.877	(877)
2	(1,000)	0.769	(769)
3	(1,000)	0.675	(675)
		2.321	(4,321)

Calculation of Annual Equivalent Value for Machine Y and Z are as follows:

AEV for machine Y = $\dfrac{\$5,510}{3.888}$

$$=\$1,417.18$$

AEV for machine Z = $\dfrac{\$4,321}{2.321}$

$$= \$1,861.7$$

Decision:
Machine Y should be chosen because it has lower AEV of cost ($1,417.18) when compared with AEV of cost ($1,861.7) of Machine Z. This is in agreement with illustration 11.1b

6. 2   Replacement and Abandonment Decisions

The method of constant replacement chains to choose between assets with different lives was discussed in the previous section. It was discussed that assets are replaced at the end of their economic lives but this is not always the case in practice.

Replacement of asset should be intelligently planned. You need to consider the economic benefits (cash inflow) of the old asset you intend to replace or abandon with a new machine you plan to accept.

Some organizations follow the practice of approving a new machine only when the existing one can no longer work properly. This is one of the most expensive policies which a business entity could follow. A professional analysis may indicate replacement of a machine when it is, say 6 years old with an improved new machine. However, if the machine is retained till when it is beyond repairs, say 17 years, the company must have been incurring extra expenditures on maintenance and losing extra profit for 11years. A company that follow this practice is likely to fold up if care is not taken as it will be unable to compete favourably with companies that adopt cost-reduction policies by adopting a systematic replacement policy and rule.

In conclusion, for a company to remain in business it should adopt a replacement policy based on economic consideration, and decide when to replace.

ILLUSTARTION 6.2

Supposing a company is operating a machine which is expected to produce net cash inflows of $2,500,000, $2,000,000, $1,500,000, $1,000,000 for the next 4 years. A new machine which is more efficient to operate and cost effective has just been introduced into the market. It is expected that the new machine will cost $7,500,000 and will generate a net cash inflow of $3,500,000 a year for six years. What should the company do?

SOLUTION

Old Machine

Years	Cash flow $'000	DF (14%)	PV $'000	AEV $'000
0		1		
1	2,500	0.877	2,193	1,831.45
2	2,000	0.769	1,538	1,831.45
3	1,500	0.675	1,013	1,831.45
4	1,000	0.592	592	1,831.45
		2.913	5,335	

New Machine

Years	Cash flow	DF (14%)	PV	AEV
	$'000		$'000	$'000
0	7,500	1	(7,500)	1,570.99
1	3,500	0.877	3,070	1,570.99
2	3,500	0.769	2,692	1,570.99
3	3,500	0.675	2,363	1,570.99
4	3,500	0.592	2,072	1,570.99
5	3,500	0.519	1,817	1,570.99
6	3,500	0.456	1,596	1,570.99
		3.888	6,108	

The table above shows that a chain of the cash flow for the new machine is equivalent to an annuity of ($6,108,000 ÷ 3.888) = $ 1,570,990 per year for the life of the machine. The old machine generates an annuity of ($5,335,000 ÷ 2.913) = $1,831,450.

Decision:

The old machine should not be replaced by the new machine because the annual equivalent value in cash inflow of the old machine ($1,831,450) is higher than that of the new machine ($1,570,990).

6.3 Inflation in Capital Budgeting

Inflation is a vital factor of the economic and must be considered in capital budgeting. It is an increase in estimate as a result of changes in price level. The impact of inflation should be correctly included in the investment in order to prevent errors. If we ignore inflation, we may end up overstating or understating our net cash flows in which case the NPVs used for decision making would be wrong.

6.3.1 Relevant Concepts

Inflation can be incorporated in capital budgeting by the usage of any of the following two concepts:

(a) Nominal rate or Money cost of capital
(b) Real rate or real cost of capital

Concept of Nominal rate or Money Cost of capital

The nominal rate is the normal cost of capital of a company which would have been calculated subject to money market rate of interest of the providers of capital or funds. It is the cost of capital that has not been adjusted for inflation. Where cash flows are inflated or are given in money terms, we should discount such cash flows using the money cost of capital.

Concept of Real Rate or Real Cost of Capital

The real rate of capital is the cost of capital that has been adjusted for inflation.

The impact of inflation in investment appraisal (capital budgeting) could be adjusted for, either in the discounting rate (cost of capital) or cash flow. The discount rate is usually determined by the market and stated in nominal terms.

However, where discount rates are expressed in real terms, they can be reversed to their nominal value through the following which is known as Fisher's effect in economic theory.

Nominal rate = (1+ Real Rate) (1+ Inflation Rate) – 1

This equation can also be used to derive the real rate of return thus:

Real Rate = $\dfrac{(1+\text{Nominal Rate})}{(1+\text{Inflation Rate})}$ - 1

If discount rate is stated in nominal terms, then cash flow must also be estimated in nominal terms. This is called consistency.

Some costs are more sensitive to inflation than others. Certain items are not affected by inflation, for instance the tax shield on depreciation (for tax purpose, depreciation is not allowed on the book value). In evaluating viability of a project, the real cash flow could be discounted at real discount rate, or the nominal cash flows discounted at the nominal rate.

Both methods will always give the same answers subject to approximation error.

ILLUSTRATION

AY Ltd. forecasts the following project cash flows in real terms, and discount at a 15% nominal rate. Should the firm invest in it if 10% rate of inflation is assumed?

	Year 0	Year 1	Year 2	Year 3
	$	$	$	$
Cash flow	20,000	7,000	10,000	6,000

SUGGESTED SOLUTION

Alternative I: Converting real cash flows to nominal terms

Years	Real Cash Flow	Workings	Nominal Cash Flows
	$	$	$
0	20,000	20,000(1)	=20,000
1	7,000	$7,000(1+0.1)^1$	=7,700
2	10,000	$10,000(1+0.1)^2$	=12,100
3	6,000	$6,000(1+0.1)^3$	=7,986

Computation of NPV

Years	Nominal Cash Flow $	D.F (15%)	PV $
0	(20,000)	1	(20,000)
1	7,700	0.8696	6,696
2	12,100	0.7561	9,149
3	7,986	0.6575	5,251
		NPV	1,096

Note: The discount rate is already in nominal term. You do not need to convert it to nominal term.

Alternative II: Converting nominal rate to real rate

$$\text{Real rate} = \frac{1 + \text{Nominal rate}}{1 + \text{Inflation rate}} - 1$$

$$= \frac{1 + 0.15}{1 + 0.1} - 1$$

$$= 4.55\%$$

Year	Cash flow $	D.F (4.55%)	PV $
0	(20,000)	1	(20,000)
1	7,000	0.9565	6,696
2	10,000	0.9149	9,149
3	6,000	0.875	5,250
		NPV	1,095

The NPV of the project is $1,095

Decision rule: The project should be accepted because the NPV of the project is positive $1,095. It can be seen that NPV in the two alternative computations are almost equal.

CHAPTER 7

CAPITAL RATIONING

Learning Objectives

After studying this chapter, you should be able to:

(i) Evaluate capital projects under single period capital rationing.

(ii) Know the meaning of multi-period capital rationing and setting up of linear programming equation.

Capital Rationing

Capital rationing arises when there are insufficient funds to execute all available and profitable projects. The inadequacy of resources to finance projects may arise due to external factors or internal constraints imposed by management.

Capital rationing situation is one in which a company does not have sufficient funds to execute worthwhile investment projects. Under this situation, a company has projects with positive NPV whose combined outlays exceed all available finance to the company for the same period.

Capital rationing is the technique for selecting projects during a period of funds restriction which normally requires the ranking of projects in a descending order of desirability and accepting them in that order until all available funds have been exhausted.

7.1 Single Period Capital Rationing

This is where restriction is for only one period. We must use profitability index to select projects where restriction is for only one year.

7.2 Profitability Index (PI)

This concept is based on the contribution per limiting factor approach. It is actually a benefit/cost analysis of projects. It can be measured by the ratio of Gross Present Value (GPV) of a project to the outlay required for the project during the year of restriction.

The formulas for calculating profitability index are mentioned below:

Profitability Index (PI)

$$= \frac{\text{Gross Present Value}}{\text{Initial Outlay}}$$

Or

$$= \frac{\text{NPV} + \text{Initial Outlay}}{\text{Initial Outlay}}$$

Steps to be taken in single period capital rationing situation are as follows:

1. Identify the year of restriction.
2. Calculate the PV and NPV of the projects (if not given).
3. Rank all projects using PI.
4. Allocate available funds to projects in a descending order of PI.
5. If a project does not require outlay during the year of restriction, its PI would be an infinite sum (NPV + 0) and such projects must be ranked first and must be selected first.

ILLUSTRATION 1

Suppose a company is faced with a problem of investing $500,000 in three projects which are all attractive and profitable @12 percent opportunity cost of capital. Which of the projects should be undertaken, given the following evaluation results?

Projects	Initial Outlay $	NPV @ 12% $

1	500,000	105,000
2	250,000	80,000
3	250,000	60,000

SUGGESTED SOLUTION

Calculation of profitability Index (PI)

$$PI = \frac{NPV + \text{Initial Outlay}}{\text{Initial Outlay}}$$

= PV/Initial Outlay
Profitability Index (P.I)

Project 1 = $\frac{\$105,000 + \$500,000}{\$500,000}$

= 1.21

Project 2 = $\frac{\$80,000 + \$250,000}{\$250,000}$

= 1.32

Project 3 = $\frac{\$60,000 + \$250,000}{\$250,000}$

= 1.24

Projects	Initial Outlay $	NPV @ 12% $	PI	Ranking using NPV	Ranking using PI
1	500,000	105,000	1.21	1	3
2	250,000	80,000	1.32	2	1
3	250,000	60,000	1.24	3	2

The above table shows that the three projects are viable and should be undertaken if there is no capital constraint, but the question states that the company has only $500,000 to invest.

Using the NPV rule, the firm will accept project 1 which has NPV of $105,000, and initial outlay of $500,000 that exhausts the available fund, but the use of PI suggests otherwise. The PI suggests the selection of project 2 and 3 which together have higher NPV of $140,000 ($80,000+ $60,000) and total initial outlay of $500,000 ($250,000 + $250,000).

Allocation of funds according to the profitability index:

	$
Available funds	500,000
Select project 2	(250,000)
	250,000
Select project 3	(250,000)
	Nil

In conclusion, where there is insufficient fund or resources to execute all the viable project, profitability index should be used in ranking the project and not NPV.

ILLUSTRATION 2

Miami Ltd. has a capital budget of $250,000 for the year to June 30, 2003. The available projects have been identified and quantified by the technical director and the works manager as listed below. The individual project's related profitability index has been computed by a financial management team and stated below:

Projects	Initial Outlay	PI
	$	

A	125,000	1.1
B	50,000	0.95
C	100,000	1.25
D	100,000	1.23
E	125,000	1.05
F	50,000	1.2
G	25,000	0.99

(a) Which projects should the company invest in?

(b) What difference would the absence of capital rationing make to your selection in "a" above?

SUGGESTED SOLUTION

(a)

Projects	Initial Outlay $	PI	Ranking
A	125,000	1.1	4th
B	50,000	0.95	7th
C	100,000	1.25	1st
D	100,000	1.23	2nd
E	125,000	1.05	5th
F	50,000	1.2	3rd
G	25,000	0.99	6th

Allocation of funds:

	$
Available funds	250,000
Allocation to project C	(100,000)
	150,000
Allocation to project D	(100,000)
	50,000
Allocation to project F	(50,000)
	-

Miami Ltd. should invest in projects C, D and F in that order of priority.

(b)

Calculation of Present Value (GPV or PV)

P.I = PV/I.O

PV= PI x I.O
Where:
 PI = profitability Index
PV = Present Value
I.O = Initial Outlay

Projects	P.I	I.O	PV= P.I X I.O	NPV= PV -I.O
		$	$	$
A	1.1	125,000	137,500	12,500
B	0.95	50,000	47,500	(2,500)
C	1.25	100,000	125,000	25,000
D	1.23	100,000	123,000	23,000
E	1.05	125,000	131,250	6,250
F	1.2			

		50,000	60,000	10,000
G	0.99	25,000	24,750	(250)

Decision rule:

If there is no capital rationing, the company should undertake all projects with positive NPV. In this case, the company should invest in all projects except projects B and G which have negative NPV.

7.3 Different Situation of Capital Rationing

The different situations of capital rationing are as follows:
(a) Where projects are divisible
(b) Where projects are indivisible
(c) Where projects are mutually dependent
(d) Where projects are mutually exclusive

Divisible Projects

In this case, there is an implicit linearity assumption between the initial outlays and the NPV's of a product. This follows from the basic assumption that fraction of a project can be undertaken. Therefore, a fractional investment in the outlay would yield a proportionate fractional return in NPV. For example, investment of 20% in the outlay, would yield 20% of NPV.

Indivisible Projects

The assumption in this case is that projects are not divisible fractions and cannot therefore be undertaken in parts. It is only in this case that there may be surplus of funds which represents the available funds after allocation.

ILLUSTRATION 3

Amazeno Ltd. is experiencing a shortage of funds for investment in the current year, when only $50,000 is available for investment. No fund shortages are foreseen thereafter. The cost of investing fund is 20%. The following projects are available:

Projects	1	2	3	4	5	6
Initial Outlay	$25,000	$40,000	$30,000	$15,000	$12,500	$20,000
Annual receipts to Perpetuity	$7,500	$10,000	$9,000	$5,000	$4,000	$5,000

You are required to advise management on the projects which you would recommend for acceptance if they were:

(a) Divisible
(b) Indivisible

SUGGESTED SOLUTION

Projects	Initial Outlay	PV	PI	Ranking
1	$25,000	$37,500	1.5	3rd
2	$40,000	$50,000	1.25	6th
3	$30,000	$45,000	1.5	4th
4	$15,000	$25,000	1.67	1st
5	$12,500	$20,000	1.6	2nd
6	$20,000	$25,000	1.25	5th

(a) Allocation of available funds where projects are divisible:

	$
Available fund	50,000
Allocation to project 4	(15,000)
	35,000
Allocation to project 5	(12,500)

	22,500
Select 90% of project 1	(22,500)
	Nil

The management should accept project 4, 5 and 90% of project 1.

(b) Allocation of available funds where projects are indivisible:

	$
Available fund	50,000
Allocation to project 4	(15,000)
	35,000
Allocation to project 5	(12,500)
	22,500
Allocation to project 6	(20,000)
Surplus funds	2,500

Since projects are indivisible, management should accept projects 4, 5 and 6.

Project 1 which is the 3rd on the ranking should be replaced by project 6 which is the next on the ranking because the initial outlay of project 1 is higher ($25,000) than the available balance of funds ($22,500) and according to the question, funds should not be allocated to the fractional part of a project.

Workings:

Calculation of present value for each project:

PV = A ×1/r

Project 1   = $7,500 x1/0.2
                 = $37,500

Project 2   = $10,000 x1/0.2
                 = $50.000

Project 3   =$9,000 x1/0.2
                 = $45,000

Project 4   = $5,000 x1/0.2
                 = $25,000

Project 5   = $4,000 x1/0.2
                 = $20.000

Project 6   = $5,000 x1/0.2
                 = $25,000

Calculation of profitability Index for each project:

PI   = PV/I.O

PI for project 1 = $37,500/$25,000
                 = 1.5

PI for project 2 = $50,000/$40,000
                 = 1.25

PI for project 3 = $45,000/30,000
                 = 1.5

PI for project 4 = $25,000/$15,000
                 = 1.67

PI for project 5 = $20,000/$12,500
                 = 1.6

PI for project 6 = $25,000/$20,000
$$= 1.25$$

Where:

PV = Present Value
A = Annual receipt from project
r = Cost of investing funds
I.O = Initial Outlay
PI =Profitability Index

Mutually Dependent Projects

In this case, acceptance of one of the mutually dependent projects automatically implies an acceptance of the remaining mutually dependent project. For example, if projects A and B are mutually dependent, it means that the two projects can either be accepted jointly or rejected together.

Mutually Exclusive Projects

In this case, an acceptance of one project group implies the rejection of all other project group. This issue can be resolved by modifying the ranking procedures and it is done as follows:

    iv. create as many groups of projects as long as they are mutually exclusive. This can be done by ensuring that each group contains only one of the mutually exclusive projects and would of course exclude the others.

    v. rank and select projects in each group

    vi. calculate the total NPVs of the selected projects in each group.

vii. the decision would be to accept projects from the groups that produce maximum total NPVs.

ILLUSTRATION 4

Jeff and Smith have just received their gratuities which amounted to $2,000,000 and they are prepared to invest in a new venture PZI Ltd. A bank has expressed the desire to grant them long-term loan of up to $10,000,000. They have presented the following investment proposals to you for financial advice.

Projects	A	B	C	D	E	F	G	H	I	J
PI	1.17	1.2	1.19	1.22	1.15	1.15	1.22	1.20	1.16	1.10
Outlay($'million)	2.00	3.00	1.50	4.00	4.00	2.00	1.00	1.50	1.00	3.00

The company expected cost of capital is 15%. Project B and C are mutually exclusive while projects A and D are mutually dependent.

(a) As a financial adviser, what projects would you recommend? Assume that fractions of a project can be undertaken.

SUGGESTED SOLUTION

Group A (includes project B but excluding project C)
Ranking

Projects	PI	I.O	PI X I.O PV	PV - I.O NPV
		$'000	$'000	$'000
G	1.22	1,000	1,220	220
H	1.2	1,500	1,800	300
B	1.2	3,000	3,600	600
A&D	1.2	6,000	7,200	1,200
I	1.16	1,000	1,160	160
F	1.15	2,000	2,300	300
E	1.15	4,000	4,600	600
J	1.1	3,000	3,300	300

Allocation of funds to the projects according to PI ranking:

	$'000	NPV $,000
Available funds	12,000	
Select project G	(1,000)	220
	11,000	
Select project H	(1,500)	300
	9,500	
Select project B	(3,000)	600
	6,500	
Select project A & D	(6,000)	1,200
	500	
Select 50% of project I	(500)	80
	Nil	2,400

The total NPV = $2,400,000
This group includes B but exclude C because the two projects are mutually exclusive while project "A" and "D" are mutually dependent.

Group B (Including project C but excluding project B)

Ranking			PI X I.O	PV - I.O
Projects	PI	I.O	PV	NPV
		$'000	$'000	$'000
G	1.22	1,000	1,220	220
H	1.2	1,500	1,800	300

A&D	1.2	6,000	7,200	1,200
C	1.19	1,500	1785	285
I	1.16	1,000	1,160	160
F	1.15	2,000	2,300	300
E	1.15	4,000	4,600	600
J	1.1	3,000	3,300	300

Allocation of funds to the projects according to PI ranking:

		NPV
	$'000	$,000
Available funds	12,000	
Select project G	(1,000)	220
	11,000	
Select project H	(1,500)	300
	9,500	
Select project A & D	(6,000)	1,200
	3,500	
Select project C	(1,500)	285
	2,000	
Select project I	(1,000)	160
	1,000	
Select 50% of project F	(1,000)	150
	Nil	2,315

The total NPV = $2,315,000

This group includes C but exclude B because the two projects are mutually exclusive while project "A" and "D" are mutually dependent.

Decision

The company is advised to choose projects G, H, B, A&D and 50% of project I (Group A) because they produced the higher NPV of $2,400,000 compared to that of group "B" of $2,315,000.

NOTE: The profitability Index for A&D is calculated as follows:

$$PI = \frac{(1.17 \times \$2\text{million}) + (1.22 \times \$4\text{million})}{\$2\text{million} + \$4\text{million}}$$

$$= \frac{\$2.34 + \$4.88\text{million}}{\$6\text{million}}$$

$$= 1.20$$

Where:

PI = profitability Index
I.O = Initial Outlay
PV = Present Value
NPV = Net Present Value

7.4 Multi-Period Capital Rationing or Funds Constraints Problems

Where capital is restricted in more than one period, a formulation of linear programming is required to select projects which will maximise the NPVs for the company.
Capital investment decision under multi-period funds constraint situations have the objectives of choosing a combination of projects

which gives the firm maximum total net present value, subject to company's resources availability.

ILLUSTRATION 1

PYZ consult has identified the following projects:

Projects	year 0 $	Year 1 $	Year 2 $
A	(100,000)	(100,000)	302,410
B	(50,000)	(100,000)	218,070
C	(200,000)	150,000	107,230

Provide a mathematical programming formulation to assist the company in choosing the most viable project if capital available for year 0 and year1 is limited to $170,000 and $80,000 respectively. Assume 5 percent cost of capital and that the projects are divisible.

SUGGESTED SOLUTION

Project A

Years	Cash Flow $	DF 5%	PV $
0	(100,000)	1	(100,000)
1	(100,000)	0.952	(95,200)
2	302,410	0.907	274,286
		NPV	79,086

Project B

Years	Cash Flow $	DF 5%	PV $
0	(50,000)	1	(50,000)
1	(100,000)	0.952	(95,200)
2	218,070	0.907	197,789
		NPV	52,589

Project C

years	Cash Flow $	DF 5%	PV $
0	(200,000)	1	(200,000)
1	150,000	0.952	142,800
2	107,230	0.907	97,258
		NPV	40,058

Maximize NPV = $79,086A + 52,589B + 40,058C

Subject to:

$100,000A + $50,000B + $200,000C ≤ $170,000

$100,000A + $100,000B ≤ $80,000 + $150,000C

A, B. C ≤ 1
A, B. C ≥ 0

Where A, B and C represent the proportion of each of the three projects which is desirable to be undertaken.

NOTE: The above equation can be solved using the computer.

7.5 Limitation of Linear/integer programming

(a) very technical

(b) can only be solved with the help of computer

(c) very costly to use when large indivisible projects are involved

(d) it assumes that future investment opportunities are known.

7.6 Limitation of Capital Rationing

The following are the limitation of capital rationing

(a) The assumption of divisibility of projects may not be possible in practice, for all projects

(b) The assumptions of linearity in initial outlay and NPV of projects may not hold because of the economies and diseconomies of scale.

(c) On many occasions, capital rationing treats projects in isolation. It does not recognise the interdependence of projects.

ILLUSTRATION 1

Phylum Plc. is a household product manufacturing company contemplating diversification as an option in its drive to improve the current low level of profitability. The company is considering, for implementation, three non-mutually exclusive and apparently viable products. The major constraints are however, the availability of sufficient funds notwithstanding the relatively low level of cost or funds. At a cost of fund of 15%, the company can only operate within a budget constraint of $15,000,000 now and a maximum of one third of this amount could be available at the beginning of the following year.

The estimated annual cash flows for the project are as follows:

Years	Project A $'000	Project B $'000	Project C $'000
0	(1,500)	(8,000)	(10,000)
1	(2,000)	(3,500)	2,000
2	1,000	6,200	2,500
3	1,500	4,600	4,500
4	2,000	3,600	4,000
5	1,500	3,400	3,000

You are required to:

(a) Formulate a linear programming model that will enable the company to select an optimal combination of the available projects.

(b) State the limitations of linear programming model in relation to project appraisal.

SOLUTION

(a)

Computation of Net Present Value (NPV) for Project A

Years	Cash Flows $'000	D.F (15%)	PV $'000
0	(1,500)	1.0000	(1,500)
1	(2,000)	0.8696	(1,739)
2	1,000	0.7561	756
3	1,500	0.6575	986
4	2,000	0.5718	1,144
5	1,500	0.4972	746
		NPV	393

Computation of Net Present Value (NPV) for Project B

Years	Cash Flows $'000	D.F (15%)	PV $'000
0	(8,000)	1.0000	(8,000)
1	(3,500)	0.8696	(3,044)
2	6,200	0.7561	4,688
3	4,600	0.6575	3,025
4	3,600	0.5718	2,058
5	3,400	0.4972	1,690
		NPV	418

Computation of Net Present Value (NPV) for Project C

Years	Project A $'000	D.F (15%)	PV $'000
0	(10,000)	1.0000	(10,000)

1	2,000	0.8696	1,739
2	2,500	0.7561	1,890
3	4,500	0.6575	2,959
4	4,000	0.5718	2,287
5	3,000	0.4972	1,492
		NPV	367

Objective: maximization of NPV

Maximize NPV = $393,000A + $418,000B + $367,000C

Where A, B and C represent the proportion of each of the three projects which is desirable to be undertaken.

Subject:

$1,500,000A + $8,000,000B + $10,000,000C $\leq$ $15,000,000

$2,000,000A + $3,500,000B - $2,000,000C $\leq$ $5,000,000

A, B, C ≤ 1

A, B, C ≥ 0

(b)
Limitations of Linear programming model are as follows:

(a) very technical

(b) can only be solved with the help of computer

(c) very costly to use when large indivisible projects are involved

(d) it assumes that future investment opportunities are known.

7.7 Summary and Conclusion

Capital rationing situation is a situation in which a company does not have enough funds or resources to finance all available viable projects. Many methods have been devised to solve both single period capital rationing and multi-period capital rationing.

CHAPTER 8

Impact of Income Tax on Capital Budgeting

Learning Objectives

After you have studied this chapter, you should be able to:
- compute after –tax cash inflow or benefit
- compute after – tax cash outflow or expense
- depreciation tax shield
- evaluate capital budgeting with income tax
- distinguish between tax savings and tax cost
- compute tax allowable depreciation

Introduction

Tax payment (income tax) is the company income tax that will be paid on the profit generated by a project being appraised. The rate of the tax is determined by government of a country.

8.1 Impact of Income Tax on Capital Allowance

Before explaining the effect of income tax on capital budgeting using a Net Present Value illustration, we need to understand three concepts namely after-tax cash inflow, after tax cash outflow and depreciation tax shield.

8.1.1 After-tax cash Inflow

Taxable cash inflows or revenues when reduced by income tax are known as after-tax cash inflows. When income tax is considered in capital investment decision, after-tax cash inflow should be used. Taxable cash inflow is cash generated by a company from the use of capital expenditure (project or equipment).
After tax-cash inflow can be calculated by using the following formula:

After tax- cash inflow = (1- Tax rate) × Taxable cash inflow or receipts

ILLUSTRATION

Smith Ltd. generates $20,000 from its operation per annum. If company income tax rate is 30%, calculate after- tax cash inflow per annum.

SOLUTION:

After-tax cash inflow = (1- Tax rate) × Taxable cash inflow

$$= (1- 0.3) × \$20,000$$

$$= \$14,000$$

8.1.2 After-tax Cash Outflow or expenses

Taxable cash outflow or expenses when reduced by income tax are known as after-tax cash outflow. Tax deductible expenses reduce taxable income and help saves income tax. Taxable cash outflow is cash spent by a company on the operation of capital expenditure (project or equipment). After-tax cash outflow can be computed using the following formula:

After-tax Cash outflow = (1- Tax Rate) × Taxable cash out flow or expenses

ILLUSTRATION

HPY Ltd. wants to acquire machinery for the production of its product. The company will incur $30,000 per annum for its operation. Given that the company income tax rate is 30%, calculate its after-tax cost per annum.

SOLUTION

After-tax cost per annum = (1- Tax Rate) × Taxable cash outflow or cost

$$= (1-0.3) \times \$30,000$$

$$= \$21,000$$

8.1.3. Depreciation Tax Shield

Depreciation is a non-cash tax allowable expense that saves income tax by reducing taxable income. The amount of tax that is saved by depreciation is known as depreciation tax shield.

The formula to compute depreciation tax shield is as follows:

Depreciation tax shield = Tax Rate × depreciation

NOTE: the depreciation above is tax allowable depreciation which is different from normal depreciation of a fixed asset.

ILLUSTRATION

The annual tax allowable depreciation of a company is $50,000 and the income tax rate is 30%. Compute depreciation tax shield.

Depreciation tax shield = Tax Rate × depreciation

$$= 30\% \times \$50,000$$

$$= \$15,000$$

8.2. Computation of Tax allowable Depreciation

It should be noted that tax allowance depreciation is allowed throughout the life span of the cost of a project or the fixed asset. It is necessary to use a straight line method of depreciation to calculate tax allowable depreciation.

ILLUSTRATION 1

A company is considering the purchase of an equipment to save its cost. The cost of the equipment is $120,000 and the expected salvage value is $15,000. The useful life of the equipment is 6years.

You are required to calculate tax allowable depreciation

SOLUTION:

Tax allowable depreciation = $\dfrac{\text{Cost of equipment}}{\text{Useful life of the equipment}}$

= $120,000/6

= $20,000

Note: The above calculation is tax allowable depreciation which is different from the calculation of normal depreciation. As far as income tax is concerned, the depreciation used is tax allowable depreciation.

8.3. Effect of Income Tax on Net Present Value of Capital Projects

We have discussed the three concepts relevant to the evaluation of capital budget where income tax is involved. We can now explain the impact of income tax on the capital investment with the aid of a comprehensive illustration. There are two ways of paying income tax. It can be paid on actual year basis (current year) or on preceding year basis (previous year)

ILLUSTRATION 1 (Where tax is paid on actual year basis or on current year)

Note: Two methods are used to compute NPV in the following illustration.

ABC Plc. is considering the acquisition of an item of machinery costing $480,000. The expected annual cash savings to be generated from the machinery is $200,000. Its useful life is 12years. The expected residual value (salvage value) is $60,000. The tax rate is 40% and discount rate is 12%.

Note:

ABC Plc. Pays tax per year in the year in which the taxable profit occurs.

The machinery is to be depreciated using straight line method.

You are required to compute NPV and advise the company whether to acquire the machinery or not.

SOLUTION

FIRST METHOD

ABC Plc.
Computation of Net Present value of ABC Plc.

	Years	Cash flow before tax	Tax effect	Cash flow after tax	D.F 12%	PV
		$		$		$
Cost of equipment	0	(480,000)		(480,000)	1	(480,000)
Annual cash savings	1 to 12	200,000	0.6	120,000	6.1944	743,328
Depreciation	1 to 12	40,000	0.4	16,000	6.1944	99,110
Residual value	12	60,000	0.6	36,000	0.2567	9,241
Net present value						371,680

The project should be accepted because it gives a positive NPV of $371,680.

Note: The residual value is regarded as cash inflow.

SECOND METHOD

Second Method for the computation of NPV when income tax is paid in the year in which profit occurs (actual or current year basis) ABC plc.

Computation of Income tax of ABC Plc.

Years	1 to 12	12
	$	$
Cash inflow :		
-Cash savings	200,000	
-Residual value		60,000
Tax allowable depreciation	(40,000)	-
Taxable income	160,000	60,000
Tax rate	× 40%	× 40%
Income tax	64,000	24,000

Computation of Net Present value of ABC Plc.

	Years	Cash flow	Tax savings	NCF	D.F(12%)	PV
		$	$	$		$
Cost	0	(480,000)	0	(480,000)	1.0000	(480,000)
Cash savings	1 - 12	200,000	(64,000)	136,000	6.1944	842,438
Residual value	12	60,000	(24,000)	36,000	0.2567	9,241
NPV						371,680

NOTE: NCF = cash flow – tax savings

Where:
NCF = Net Cash Flow
D.F = Discount Factor
PV = Present value

The project should be accepted because it gives a positive NPV of $371,680.

NOTE: It can be seen that the two methods give the same NPV of $371,680

WORKINGS:

a) Calculation of tax allowable depreciation = $480,000/12

$$= \$40,000$$

b) Calculation of annuity factor (D.F 12%)

Annuity factor $= \dfrac{(1 - (1+ r)^{-n})}{r}$

$$= \dfrac{(1 - (1+ 0.12)^{-12})}{0.12}$$

$$= \dfrac{(1 - (1/1.12)^{12})}{0.12}$$

$$= \dfrac{(1 - 0.256675)}{0.12}$$

$$= 6.194375$$

$$= 6.1944$$

c) Calculation of Discount factor for year 12;

Discount factor for year 12 $= (1+0.12)^{-12}$

$$= 0.2567$$

ILLUSTRATION 2

JJ Plc. is considering whether to acquire new equipment or not. The cost of the equipment is $1,000,000 and it will achieve annual sales of $800,000. The expenditure per annum is $500,000. The useful life of the equipment is 4years and the expected realisable value at the end of the 4th year is $400,000. Tax rate is 35%. Tax allowable depreciation is at the rate of 25% on a straight line basis of all fixed assets. The company cost of capital for the project is 16%.

Note: Assume that income tax is paid in the current year of the profit.
Required: Compute NPV of the project

SOLUTION

FIRST METHOD

JJ Plc.
Computation of Net Present Value (NPV)

	Years	Cash flow before tax	Tax Effect	Cash flow after tax	D.F 16%	PV
		$		$		$
Cost of equipment	0	(1,000,000)		(1,000,000)	1	(1,000,000)
Annual cash sales	1 - 4	800,000	0.65	520,000	2.7982	1,455,064
Depreciation	1 - 4	250,000	0.35	87,500	2.7982	244,843
Expenditure	1 - 4	(500,000)	0.65	(325,000)	2.7982	(909,415)
Residual value	4	400,000	0.65	260,000	0.5523	143,598
Net present value						(65,911)

The Net Present Value of the project is -$65,911. This project should be rejected because it has negative NPV.

SECOND Method

JJ Plc.
Computation of Income Tax

	1	2	3	4	4
	$	$	$	$	
Annual Sales	800,000	800,000	800,000	800,000	400,000
Expenditure	(500,000)	(500,000)	(500,000)	(500,000)	-
Assessable profit	300,000	300,000	300,000	300,000	
Tax allowable depreciation	(250,000)	(250,000)	(250,000)	(250,000)	
Taxable profit	50,000	50,000	50,000	50,000	400,000
Tax rate	35%	35%	35%	35%	35%
Income Tax	17,500	17,500	17,500	17,500	140,000

Computation of Net Present value (NPV)

	Year	Cash flow	Income tax/Tax costs	NCF	D.F(16%)	PV
		$	$	$		$
Cost	0	(1,000,000)	0	(1,000,000)	1.0000	(1,000,000)
Annual sales	1 - 4	300,000	(17,500)	282,500	2.7982	790,492
Residual value	4	400,000	(140,000)	260,000	0.5523	143,598
NPV						(65,911)

Decision:

The Net Present Value of the project is -$65,911. This project should be rejected because it has negative NPV.

It can be seen that the two computed NPV from the two methods give -$65,911

ILLUSTRATION 3

Assume that you are given the same question in illustration 2 but JJ Plc. pays income tax one year in arrears.

	1	2	3	4	4
	$	$	$	$	
Annual Sales	800,000	800,000	800,000	800,000	
Residual value					400,000
Expenditure	(500,000)	(500,000)	(500,000)	(500,000)	-
Assessable profit	300,000	300,000	300,000	300,000	
Tax allowable depreciation	(250,000)	(250,000)	(250,000)	(250,000)	
Taxable profit	50,000	50,000	50,000	50,000	400,000
Tax rate	× 35%	× 35%	× 35%	× 35%	× 35%
Income Tax	17,500	17,500	17,500	17,500	140,000

NOTE: income tax to be paid in year 5 is the addition of income tax in year 4 and income tax on residual value (balancing charge) in year 4. $17,500 + $140,000 = $157,500

Computation of Net Present Value(NPV)

years	Cash flow	Income tax/Tax cost	NCF	D.F (16%)	PV
	$	$	$		$
0	(1,000,000)	-	(1,000,000)	1	(1,000,000)

1	300,000	-	300,000	0.8621	258,630
2	300,000	(17,500)	282,500	0.7432	209,954
3	300,000	(17,500)	282,500	0.6407	180,998
4	300,000	(17,500)	282,500	0.5523	156,025
4	400,000	-	400,000	0.5523	220,920
5	-	(157,500)	(157,500)	0.4761	(74,986)
			NPV		(48,459)

Decision:

The project should be rejected because the NPV shows Negative value of -$48,459

NOTE:

Cost of capital is always the cost of capital after tax except it is stated on the question that it is cost of capital before tax.

8.4 Relevant Concepts in Income Tax and Capital Investment Decision

8.4.1 Difference between Tax Written Down Value and Expected Sales Value of Capital Expenditure (fixed asset)

Tax written down value (TWDV) of an asset (qualifying capital expenditure) is the amount that is available after tax allowable depreciation has be deducted from the asset. It may be available every year and at the end of the whole useful life of the asset. TWDV has zero value almost all the time, but where reducing balance of depreciation is used to compute tax allowable depreciation, it may be greater than Zero.

Expected sales value or salvage value (residual value) of an asset (qualifying capital expenditure) is the market value or saleable value of an asset at the time of disposal or at the end of its useful life.

The main difference between TWDV of an asset (qualifying capital expenditure) and its residual value is that the TWDV is the cost of the asset remaining in the book at the time of disposal of the asset or at the end of useful life of the asset while residual value is the saleable value or sale price of the asset at the time of disposal or at the end of the useful life of the asset.

8.4.2 Balancing Adjustments

Balancing adjustments arise where an asset (a qualifying capital expenditure) is disposed off. It is classified into balancing charge and balancing allowance.

Balancing Charge

Balancing Charge is the amount by which the sale price or saleable value of an asset is greater than its TWDV. This written down value is actually believed to be the actual value of that asset for the purposes of taxation. Therefore, the balancing charge will be considered as profit and it will be taxable.

For example, assume that TWDV of an asset is 0 and the sale price or residual value of the asset is $15,000. The balancing charge will be $15,000 – 0, which is equal to $15,000. If income tax rate is 30%. The tax on balancing charge will be ($15,000 -0) 30% = $4,500. This tax on balancing charge is referred to as **tax cost** and it is an addition to income tax that will be paid to the revenue authority.

Balancing Allowance

Balancing allowance is the amount by which the sale price or residual value of an asset is less than its TWDV. For example, assume that the TWDV of an asset is $12,000 and its residual value is $9,000. Calculate the balancing allowance.

Balancing allowance = Residual value - TWDV
$$= \$9,000 - \$12,000$$
$$= - \$3,000$$

The balancing allowance is $3,000

Assume that, tax rate is 30% .The tax on the balancing allowance will be $3,000 × 30% = $900. This tax on balancing allowance is referred to as tax savings and it is a deduction from income tax.

8.4.3 Investment Allowance

Investment allowance is granted in respect of a new qualified capital expenditure to induce investment in certain sector of the economy.

CHAPTER 9

Lease and Buy Decisions

Learning Objective

After this chapter, you should be able to:

- Understand the appropriate cost of capital to be used for lease and buy decision
- Know when to lease and when to buy
- Know how a tax allowable depreciation affects lease or buy decision
- Know how an income tax affects lease or buy decision

A Lease is a contract by which one party conveys land, property, and services to another for a specified time, usually in return for a periodic payment.

According to a BusinesDictionary, a lease is a written or implied contract by which an owner (the lessor) of a specific asset (such as a parcel of land, building, equipment, or machinery) grants a second party (the lessee) the right to its exclusive possession and use for a specific period and under specified conditions, in return for specified periodic rental or lease payments.

Lease and buy decisions are usually mutually exclusive, hence the usage of incremental approach will quicken the rate of solving problems in this area. Tax allowable depreciations (capital allowances) would substantially have an impact on lease and buy decisions, therefore, the earlier explained adjustments on tax allowable depreciation and balancing adjustments are expected under a lease or buy decision with particular reference to the buy option. However, in financial management, it is assumed that an operating lease arrangement will not enjoy tax allowable depreciation. It is assumed that leases under capital investment decision are regarded as either operating leases or finance leases.

9.1 Factors affecting Lease or Buy Decisions

The following factors need to be considered when lease or buy decisions are involved.

a) Liquidity

(i) Do we have enough funds now to buy the asset instead of leasing it?

(ii) Are we going to have sufficient funds in the future to meet a lease obligation?

(b) Off balance sheet financing: leasing will be more attractive than borrowing or buying if a company is already highly geared.

(c) Availability of spare parts and ease of maintenance: Some lease contracts involve maintenance clauses. It will be more economical to allow lessor who has more knowledge about the asset to handle maintenance and the importation of spare parts of the asset.

(d) Beneficial owner: It is advisable not to lease specialized equipment or accommodation.

(e) Changes in technology or obsolescence: Leasing may become very attractive if the asset is exposed to regular changes in technology. For example, leasing is very common in sophisticated industries such as aircrafts and computer industries.

(f) Distribution in production: This will lead to losses if the lessor repossesses the asset for any reason.

(g) Changes in taxation rate: This factor can also affect a lease or buy decision.

(h) Inflation: This may affect lease or buy decisions in terms of changes in prices. Inflation may have substantial impact on buy decisions while it may not have an impact on lease decision.

9.2 Relevant Assumptions

The following important assumptions may be used as guides in making lease or buy decisions:

Choice of Cost of Capital

(i) Nature of cost of capital: if the company is in a taxable position, use the after tax cost of capital. The after tax cost of capital is that cost of capital that has been directly or indirectly adjusted for taxation. Tax adjustments are considered direct if tax has been recognised during the specific computation of cost of capital. It is indirect if the cost of capital is adjusted using the following formula: After tax cost of capital = Cost of capital $\times$ (1 – Tax Rate).

For example, if cost of capital is 20% and tax rate is 30%. Calculate after tax cost of capital.

Solution:
After tax cost of capital = 20% $\times$ (1- 0.3)
$$= 14\%$$
Where a company is not in a taxable position, we should use before tax cost of capital. A company is in a taxable position if it is required by law to pay tax during its normal operation. If a company is currently making losses and therefore not paying taxes, it does not mean that the company is not in a taxable position. The loss position of a company is only considered as a tax relief.

(ii) Specific cost of capital: The choice of cost of capital to be used for either the lease or buy decision is determined by the source of finance or by reference to the nature of cash flow. If the source of finance is specified, we should use the specific cost of finance. For example, if the source of finance is a borrowing of loan, we should use cost of borrowing the loan.

9.3 Nature of Cash Flows

Cash flows are considered certain if they do not vary directly with changes in sales and production, and if they do not fluctuate over time. For example, cash flows from rentals, lease, hire purchases are considered certain. On the contrary, cash flows are considered uncertain if they are dependent on the level of activities of the company.

9.4 Asset bought on lease

A lease is an agreement whereby the lessor transfers to the lessee in return for a rent, the right to use an asset for an agreed period of time.

A lease is of two types; finance lease and operating lease. This distinction is very important because the nature of the lease will resolve the question of who claims capital allowance between a lessor and a lessee.

In case of operating lease, the property reverts to a lessor after the period of the lease. It is the lessor that continues to record the asset as its own in his or her own books, depreciating them and claiming capital allowances on them. Rentals paid by the lessee are allowable expenses only to be charged against the income, provided the leased asset is used wholly, exclusively and necessarily for the business. Additional expenditure properly incurred for the maintenance of the leased asset is also an allowable expense.

In case of finance lease, the lease is normally over the useful life of an asset and rewards and risks of ownership are substantially transferred to the lessee. The lessee is entitled to claim capital allowances normally allowed to an owner of such equipment.

ILLUSTRTION 1

LILI Ltd. intends to obtain the use of an asset, but is uncertain of the best financing method to be employed. The financing methods under consideration are:

(a) To borrow and purchase the asset: borrowing would cost 12% before tax, the current competitive market rate for debt. The asset would cost $90,000 to purchase and will have a guaranteed salvage value of $10,000 in five years. Expenditure on the asset qualifies for tax allowable depreciation (capital allowance) at 25% per annum on the reducing balance method.

(b) To lease the asset, two types of leases are being considered, the details are:

Payment to be made

Year	Lease A $	Lease B $
0	20,000	4,000
1	20,000	8,000
2	20,000	16,000
3	20,000	30,000
4	20,000	50,000

If the asset is leased, the entire salvage value will accrue to the lessor. The firm weighted average cost of capital is 15%. Advise on the best method of financing the use of the asset if the firm is:

(a) Subject to company tax at 35% with one year delay and has large taxable profits

(b) Permanently in a non-taxable position.

SOLUTION

BUY DECISION

	a	B	a+b		
		Tax			
Years	Cash Flow	savings/cost	NCF	D.F (7.8%)	PV
	$	$	$		$
0	(90,000)		(90,000)	1.0000	(90,000)
1	-		-	0.9276	-
2	-	7,875	7,875	0.8605	6,776
3	-	5,906	5,906	0.7983	4,715
4	-	4,430	4,430	0.7405	3,280
5	-	3,320	3,320	0.6869	2,281
5	10,000		10,000	0.6869	6,869
6		6,467	6,467	0.6372	4,121
			NPV		(61,958)

LEASE A

	a	b	a + b		
		Tax		D.F	
Years	Cash Flow	savings/cost	NCF	(7.8%)	NPV
	$	$	$		$
0	(20,000)		(20,000)	1.0000	(20,000)
1	(20,000)	7,000	(13,000)	0.9276	(12,059)
2	(20,000)	7,000	(13,000)	0.8605	(11,187)
3	(20,000)	7,000	(13,000)	0.7983	(10,378)
4	(20,000)	7,000	(13,000)	0.7405	(9,627)
5		7,000	7,000	0.6869	4,808
			NPV		(58,441)

Lease B

Years	a Cash Flow $	b Tax savings/cost $	a + b NCF $	D.F (7.8%)	NPV $
0	(4,000)		(4,000)	1.0000	(4,000)
1	(8,000)	1,400	(6,600)	0.9276	(6,122)
2	(16,000)	2,800	(13,200)	0.8605	(11,359)
3	(30,000)	5,600	(24,400)	0.7983	(19,479)
4	(50,000)	10,500	(39,500)	0.7405	(29,250)
5		17,500	17,500	0.6869	12,021
			NPV		(58,188)

Decision Rule:

Lease B should be selected because it has lowest investment cost or present value of cost.

WORKINGS:

1. After-tax cost of capital $= 12\% \, (1 - 35\%)$
$$= 7.8\%$$

2. Computation of capital allowance:

		$
Year 1	Cost	90,000
	Tax allowable depreciation(25% × 90000)	(22,500)
Year 2	Written Down Value (WDV)	67,500
	Tax allowable depreciation (25% × 67500)	(16,875)
Year 3	Written Down Value (WDV)	50,625
	Tax allowable depreciation (25% × 50,625)	(12,656)

Year 4	Written Down Value (WDV)	37,969

Note:
Tax allowable depreciation cannot be claimed under operating lease. This type of lease is an operating lease. This fact is gotten from the question above that stated that if the asset is leased, the entire salvage value will accrue to the lessor. It means that the asset cannot be transferred to the lessee.

	Tax allowable depreciation (25% × 37,969)	(9,492)
Year 5	Written Down Value (WDV)	28,477
	Tax allowable depreciation (25% × 28,477)	(7,119)
Year 6	Written Down Value (WDV)	21,358

3. Computation of Tax Savings on Buy Decision

Years	1	2	3	4	5	5
	$	$	$	$	$	$
Cash Flow:						
Cash sales	-	-	-	-	-	-
Residual value	-	-	-	-	-	10,000
Total cash flow	-	-	-	-	-	10,000
Tax allowable dep.	(22,500)	(16,875)	(12,656)	(9,492)	(7,119)	-
WDV	-	-	-	-	-	(21,357)
	(22,500)	(16,875)	(12,656)	(9,492)	(7,119)	(11,357)
Tax rate	× 35%	× 35%	× 35%	× 35%	× 35%	× 35%
Tax savings	(7,875)	(5,906)	(4,430)	(3,322)	(2,492)	(3,975)

Note: Tax savings in year 6 is an addition of two tax savings in year 5 ($2,492 +3,975)

4. Computation of tax savings for LEASE A

Years	0	1	2	3	4
	$	$	$	$	$
Cash Flow	(20,000)	(20,000)	(20,000)	(20,000)	(20,000)
Tax	× 35%	× 35%	× 35%	× 35%	× 35%
Tax savings	(7,000)	(7,000)	(7,000)	(7,000)	(7,000)

5. Computation of Tax Savings for LEASE B

Years	0	1	2	3	4
	$	$	$	$	$
Cash Flow	4,000	8,000	16,000	30,000	50,000
Tax	× 35%	× 35%	× 35%	× 35%	× 35%
Tax savings	1,400	2,800	5,600	10,500	17,500

Note: Tax allowable depreciation cannot be claimed under operating lease. This lease is an operating lease. This fact is gotten from the question above which stated that if the asset is leased, the entire salvage value will accrue to the lessor. It means that the asset cannot be transferred to the lessee.

REVIEW QUESTIONS

Question 1

(a) Distinguish between soft capital rationing and hard capital
rationing, and give reasons why a company may face either
of them.

(b) PZ Plc. is considering its investment program for years 2005
and 2006. The following investment opportunities are
available:

Projects	1/1/2005	1/1/2006	1/1/2007	1/1/2008	NPV
	$'000	$'000	$'000	$'000	$'000
A	(30)	(90)	120	70	30.6
B	(60)	(15)	90	40	23.1
C	(24)	(24)	40	40	12.7
D	(15)	(30)	90	40	54.9

The following assumptions were made about the projects:

(i) No other project was expected to be available at January 1 of
year 2005 and 2006.
(ii) None of the above projects could be delayed.
(iii) A fraction of a project could be undertaken and no project
could be undertaken more than once.

PZ Plc. is financed entirely by common stocks (ordinary shares) and
has a cost of capital of 14 per cent. It is the policy of the company to
invest surplus funds in a bank deposit at an annual interest rate of 8
per cent.

You are required to:

(i) Select projects to undertake and their financial benefits if capital is expected to be freely available at 14 per cent during all future periods.

(ii) Show how your answer to (i) would vary if the available capital for investment was limited to $71,500 at January 1, 2005 but was unlimited thereafter.

(iii) Provide a mathematical programming formulation which would assist the directors of PZ Plc. in choosing investment projects if capital available at January 1, 2005 was limited to $71,500 , capital available at January 1, 2006 was limited to $50,000 and capital was available thereafter without limit at 14% per annum.

Question 2

Myth Brothers International Company is considering the modernization of a machine originally costing $500,000. It has zero book value. However the machine is in a good working condition and can be sold for $250,000. Two choices are available to the company: to refurbish the existing machine at a cost of $1,800,000 or replace it with a new one at a cost of $2,100,000 with an installation cost of $300,000.

The refurbished machine as well as the new machine would have a six-year life with no salvage value. The projects, after-tax cash flows under the various alternatives are:

Years	Existing $'000	Refurbished $'000	New $'000
1	2,000	2,600	2,800
2	2,500	2,900	3,400
3	3,100	3,800	3,700
4	3,600	400	4,500
5	4,100	4,500	4,800

| 6 | 5,000 | 5,400 | 5,600 |

The cost of capital is 12 per cent.

You are required to:

Advise the company as to whether it should refurbish the existing machine or replace it with a new machine.

SOLUTIONS

Solution to question 1

(a)

Soft capital rationing which is also known as artificial capital rationing, is a self-imposed restriction to capital budgeting. It is normally caused by internal factors.

Soft capital rationing may arise as a result of any of the following:

- Management may be reluctant to issue additional share capital because of the fear that outsiders may gain control of the business or dilution of the ownership
- Management may be unwilling to issue additional share capital because it may lead to dilution in earnings per share.
- Management may not want to raise additional debt capital because it does not want to be committed to large fixed interest payments.

Hard Capital rationing which is also known as real capital rationing, is an externally imposed restriction to capital budgeting. It is normally caused by external factors and may arise as a result of any of the following:

- Raising money through the stock market may not be possible if share prices are depressed.
- There may be restrictions on bank lending due to government control.
- Financial institutions may consider an organization too risky to be granted further loan facilities.

(b)

(i)   If capital is to be freely available at 14 per cent per annum during all future periods, all the projects with positive Net present values should be selected as follows:

Projects	NPV
	$'000
A	30.6
B	23.1
C	12.7
D	54.9
Total NPV	121.3

(ii)   If capital is restricted to $71,500 in year 2005, but unlimited thereafter, the selection will be based on profitability index (PI) of each project.

Formula for the calculation of profitability index:

$$PI = PV/IO$$

Calculation of profitability index for each project:

Where:
PI = Profitability Index
PV = Present Value
IO = Initial Outlay

$$\text{Project A} = \frac{30.6 + 30}{30}$$

$$= 2.02$$

$$\text{Project B} = \frac{23.1 + 60}{60}$$

$$= 1.39$$

$$\text{Project C} \quad = \frac{12.7 + 24}{24}$$

$$= 1.53$$

$$\text{Project D} \quad = \frac{54.9 + 15}{15}$$

$$= 4.66$$

The ranking of the projects are as follows:

Project	PI	Ranking
A	2.02	2nd
B	1.39	4th
C	1.53	3rd
D	4.66	1st

The allocation of the available funds are as follows:

Project	Ranking	Funds utilization $'000
		71.5
D	1st	-15
		56.5
A	2nd	-30
		26.5
C	3rd	-24
		2.5
B	4th	-2.5
		0

Mathematical Programming:

Let: a represent the proportion of project A to be undertaken
b represent the proportion of project B to be undertaken
c represent the proportion of project C to be undertaken

d represent the proportion of project D to be undertaken

Using Linear Programming (LP) method, we shall seek to:

Maximize NPV = 30.6a + 23.1b + 12.7c + 54.9d

Subject to:

30a + 60b + 24c +15d ≤ $71.5

90a + 15b + 24c + 30d ≤ $50

a, b, c, d ≤ 1

a, b. c. d ≥ 0

Note:
   1) The values above are in thousands.

   2) Since all the projects have positive Net present values, and
      there is divisibility of a project, there would be no surplus
      funds at January 1, 2005.

Solution to question 2

Appraisal of refurbishment of old machine

Cost of refurbishment = $1,800,000

Computation of NPV of refurbishment

Years	Incremental Cash flow $'000	Discount Factor (12%)	PV $'000
0	(1,800)	1.0000	(1,800.00)
1			

	600	0.8929	535.74
2	400	0.7972	318.88
3	700	0.7118	498.26
4	(3,200)	0.6355	(2,033.60)
5	400	0.5674	226.96
6	400	0.5066	202.64
		NPV	(2,051.12)

Computation of NPV of new machine

Years	Incremental Cash flow $'000	Discount Factor	PV $'000
0	(2,150)	1.0000	(2,150.00)
1	800	0.8929	714.32
2	900	0.7972	717.48
3	600	0.7118	427.08
4	900	0.6355	571.95
5	700	0.5674	397.18
6	600	0.5066	303.96
		NPV	981.97

Decision: Replace with a new machine as it has positive NPV as against negative NPV for refurbishment.

WORKINGS:

Calculation of incremental cash flow of refurbished and existing machine

Years	a Refurbished machine cash flow $'000	b Existing machine cash flow $'000	a-b Incremental Cash flow $'000
1	2,600	2,000	600
2	2,900	2,500	400
3	3,800	3,100	700
4	400	3,600	(3,200)
5	4,500	4,100	400
6	5,400	5,000	400

Computation of incremental cash flow of new machine

Years	A New $'000	B Existing Machine cash flow $'000	a-b Incremental Cash flow $'000
1	2,800	2,000	800
2	3,400	2,500	900
3	3,700	3,100	600
4	4,500	3,600	900
5	4,800	4,100	700
6	5,600	5,000	600

Appraisal of replacement with a new machine

	$
Cost of new machine	2,100,000
Installation cost	300,000
	2,400,000
Less Disposal value of old machine	(250,000)
Net cost of the new machine	2,150,000

Note: The cost of the old machine is not included in the computation of the NPV because it is an historical cost (sunk cost).

References:

Toye Adelaja (2016) Budgeting and Budgetary Control

ICAN (2009) Strategic Financial Management

www.accountinghour.com